Thoughts From a Line at the DMV

Thoughts from a Line at the DMV

Poems by

Jim Landwehr

© 2019 Jim Landwehr. All rights reserved.
This material may not be reproduced in any form, published,
reprinted, recorded, performed, broadcast,
rewritten or redistributed without
the explicit permission of Jim Landwehr.
All such actions are strictly prohibited by law.

Cover design: Shay Culligan
Cover art: W. Jack Savage

ISBN: 978-1-950462-35-3

Kelsay Books Inc.

kelsaybooks.com

502 S 1040 E, A119
American Fork, Utah 84003

This book is dedicated to my longtime friend, Pat Judd,
who not only appreciates poetry, but who gets me.

Acknowledgments

I'd like to thank the Mighty Monday Nighters at the AllWriters' Workplace and Workshop for their friendship and critiques. Together we struggled, encouraged one another, and lamented the alignment of words we've been given, questioning whether they are truly our voices or just fake news.

In addition, I'd like to thank Kathrine, Cristina, Mary Jo, Kathie, Kirsten and Kerry for their ongoing encouragement. They are kinder with their words than I ever deserve. I also have to thank the brilliance of Richard Brautigan whose work fuels my love for poetry. A shout of gratitude to the board and citizens of the Village of Wales, Wisconsin for granting me the honor of serving as Poet Laureate for these past couple years. And, of course, my wife Donna, who always supports my writing pursuits, and understands better than anyone my need to pen my thoughts.

With extreme graciousness, I thank Karen and the staff at Kelsay Books for believing in my work and bringing it to the wider world. And to W. Jack Savage for his amazing artwork which serves as the cover for this collection. Finally, I would have to give credit to those journals and magazines that were kind enough to publish my work prior to this book.

~

"Hold The Line"—published in *Bramble Lit Mag*
"Student Body"—published in *Linnet's Wings*
"It Matters"—published in *Bramble Lit Mag*
"Bill Of Health"—published in *Red Cedar Review*
"Gunless Wonder"—published in the *East Lansing Festival Poetry Press*
"Terestrially Adjusted"—published in *Red Cedar Review*
"ReCreation"—published in *The Wild Word*

"Unqualified"—published in *Cirrus Poetry Review and nominated for Best of the Net*
"Coffee and Crazy"—published in *From The Edge Poetry Magazine*
"A Triage Of Words"—published in *Tree House Arts*
"A Drop In The Bucket"—published in *Bramble Lit Mag*
"Talking Around The Problem"—published in *Rising Phoenix Press*
"Heaven"—published in *Your Daily Poem*
"The Face Of Rain"—published in *The Wisconsin Fellowship of Poets Calendar*
"Giants"—published in *Portage Magazine*
"Flattened"—published in *Tiny Spoon Issue 1*
"Quiet One"—published in *Poets To Come Anthology*
"This is a Test"—winner of the Rosebud Magazine Poetry Contest

Contents

Trout Fishing in Middle America	15
Inattentive Living	16
The DMV (Department of Motor Vehicles)	17
Brash	20
Lumberhacks	21
Hold the Line	23
Dog Years	24
Student Body	26
Oceanside	27
BadAss Daddy	28
It Matters	29
Bill of Health	30
Gunless Wonder	32
Purgatorial Prose	34
Sixteen Times Four	35
Terrestrially Adjusted	36
The Other Dean's List	37
Wading In	38
ReCreation	39
Unqualified	40
Unwelcome	42
Coffee and Crazy	43
Created	45
Continental Fake	46
Character and Charm	48
Asocial Media	49
A Triage of Words	50
Sign Here, Here and Here	51
A Drop in the Bucket	52

Disorderly Lives	53
Count to Five	54
Filling Space	55
Downriver	56
Incarnaturalization	58
Talking Around the Problem	59
Heaven	60
Grand	61
Son	62
Family Medicine	63
Fighting Words	64
The Face of Rain	65
Giants	66
A Look Around	67
Dreamscape	69
Flattened	70
Quiet One	71
House Arrest	72
The Fourth of July before the End of the World	73
Shelf Life	75
Lion	76
This Is a Test	77

Trout Fishing in Middle America

(With reverence to Richard Brautigan)

I went trout fishing in Middle America today
it was a break from my writing
or my writing was a break from my fishing
the jury's still out.

I don't trout fish in Middle America often
but my homey little cabin retreat
was cursed by a homey little trout stream
that beckoned me repeatedly as I typed away.

I found trout fishing in Middle America difficult
I averaged eighteen snags per dozen casts
including the same log ninety-three times
the log laughed at me as I thrashed and cursed.

I'd heard that trout in Middle America are savvy
they'd seen open water fishing hacks like me
disguise ourselves as trout fishermen
only to return home troutless and defeated.

I trout fished Middle America with fury and malice
and, seventeen casts before I was going to quit,
a low-achieving, flunkie fish took my spinner
and started running like a Jamaican trout on visa.

I set the Jamaican trout from Middle America free
after a discussion on how to spot fake trout fishermen
he thanked me and swam smartly away
carefully avoiding the laughing log.

Inattentive Living

Attention is a lost art in this land
of the here and now, now hear this,
look at this, listen to that, read the other
while doing something unrelated
to any of it, especially the this
and maybe the that, or the other thing
that was forgotten in the hustle
and bustle or the wrestle and tussle
with the moments and hours
when appointments forgotten
were remembered, but it was already
too late to show up or bring up
throw up or maybe even grow up
to see that time is an imaginary
construct meant for people with
watches and alarm clocks and moments
to set them and change them,
wrists to wear them,
walls to hang them, or to live within
or tear down in the spirit
of equality and graciousness
because he is the same as she
and her sister is equals with
your brother and each of us
is here to listen and learn
or maybe hear and quickly forget
but then remember and recall
that we must open our eyes
to see this, or cup our ears to
hear that, or turn the music down
to hear any of it, tune our brains in
to pick up on the nuances
while paying rapt and focused
attention to what is right in front of us.

The DMV (Department of Motor Vehicles)

- One of the things I fear more than a root canal, is being required to pay a visit to the DMV.

- I often consider driving a car with an untransferred title or with expired tabs in order to avoid entering the doors of the DMV.

- Sometimes I have to go to the DMV to renew something, correct an issue, prove that I am still me, or that I still own my car and that it runs okay. I hate those days.

- The DMV near me has a very sophisticated numbering system. Yesterday I was number J620. It made me feel like a human bingo chip.

- I wonder why our DMV doesn't just give everyone ordinary numbers? It's so strange. Maybe the employees are secretly playing bingo.

- The DMV is a busy place. They had to hire two people just to tell bingo chip people like me what line to stand in after standing in line waiting to talk to them.

- One time I went to the DMV, and there wasn't a long, slow-moving line of people. Oh, wait, yes there was.

- Trips to the DMV always require a trip back home to get a form that I need, or some sort of better proof that I am me. This means going to the DMV twice in a day. This is like getting a root canal on a Monday morning in February.

- Filling out paper forms at the DMV is like taking a high school chemistry test, and if you get an answer wrong, you have to go back to the end of the line. I fail a lot of chemistry tests.

- Nobody smiles at the DMV. This is because most of the bingo chip people are only there because they have to prove they can still drive without killing other bingo chips.

- I think the cameras at the DMV have special filters on them that make men look like pedophiles and women look like psychotic meth addicts that haven't slept for three days.

- In an effort to keep the fake ID black market guys on their toes, the DMV makes new drivers licenses with three and sometimes four pictures of the driver on them. Now they look like an ID for a gang of pedophiles or psychotic, sleepless meth addicts.

- An amplified, automated voice calls the human bingo numbers to approach a specific counter at the DMV. The poor, real-person lady calling people for license pictures was not amplified. She had to yell!

- Once when I went to the DMV to renew my license, the clerk told me to read the bottom line to prove I could see. When I struggled to see the letters, the clerk waited for a second and then said, "Out loud, please!" I think she thought I was an idiot. I wasn't. I was just a blind bingo chip person.

- The DMV has rules that if you have a motorcycle learner's permit you can't have passengers, or ride on the freeway, or ride after dark. When I had mine, I once gave a girl a ride…on the freeway…at night…after I'd been drinking. The DMV guys never even knew.

Brash

Her voice is a blend of
bagpipes, fireworks and
a locomotive pile up.
It matches her personality
a mix of salt and vinegar
jalapenos and bleach.
She scorches like a tire fire
burning in Cleveland
spreading her ashen passion
for purpose and meaning
like a Jehovah's witness
at the doorstep of my life.
She dresses in fashion
that is part gypsy
a healthy dose of
lion tamer with a
dash of bluegrass fiddler.
Her clothes shout
Pay attention to me!
Makeup is not her thing
there is no part of her
that is made up
she's as real as lemon drops
and toll booths and the
San Francisco fog.

Lumberhacks

Not one of us was a lumberjack
or even an arborist.
What we had was
a geographer,
an electrical engineer
a foundry worker
a couple of chainsaws
a ladder
and good insurance.
The goals were simple.
First was to take down
a forty-foot tree.
Second was
to avoid dismemberment,
paralyzing falls,
or a shed-crushing drop.
The foundry worker
led the project
the electrical engineer
who owned the trees
was a nervous wreck
and the geographer
was big on
unsolicited advice and
gravitational speculation.
When it was his turn to cut
the geographer was penalized
by the foundry worker
twice for wielding
dangerous chainsaw
cutting techniques.
He was a map guy

by trade
for good reason,
apparently.
Eventually, they found a rythym
a symphony of
sawdust, noise
and two-stroke exhaust.
After some work
they felled that tree
kicked its ash
separated its limbs
not their own
and spared the lives of
a geographer, an engineer
and a foundry worker.

Hold the Line

It starts so innocently
"…please hold"
And before I can say
"I don't want to"
I'm patched into
the middle of a
bad Kenny G solo or
scratchy George Winston
piano melodies
or any number
of solos by unnamed,
middle-of-the-road
jazz guitarists.
Some might use this
time to meditate
to soul search
or make grocery lists.
Not me.
I use it to
search for the minutes
of my life
I wasted
lost forever
somewhere
in the midst of
this phone call.

Dog Years

Somewhere on the time
space continuum
I have come to a certain age
of caring for aging pets
two cats in their mid teens
on the human scale
which works out to
seventy-six cat years
and I think one has
feline diabetes and
isn't telling us
or maybe we're
not telling him
we're just in denial
because if it comes down
to insulin for him or
or paying the light bill
the answer lies in my
brightly lit future.

My Terrier is not exactly
a pup anymore either
after long naps he rises
and hobbles like his old man
hitching his giddyup
popping joints back
into assigned sockets
while breathing with
breath that smells
like a 30 day dead carp
due to some dental

issues—again like his old man
if only they made
mouthwash for dogs
or for the sake of
old dog owners.

Student Body

In an American history class
sits a ten-year old boy
focused on the sheen of
the brunette hair on
the girl the next desk over.
It cascades down her neck
falling like so much water
and crashing on the rocks
of her shoulders below.
Combed in fine columns
a hair thick, each one
in exactly the right place.
If he inhales deeply enough
he can smell her shampoo
her scent smooth like velvet.
If only she saw him.
If only he were not so shy,
they might become something
the two of them and her hair.
As the teacher drones on
about the winter at Valley Forge
the boy dreams about
the valley of her neck
knowing that these thoughts
are not condoned and
more likely deviant
sparking his own revolution.

Oceanside

We met the surf in Oceanside just before noon
Midwesterners trying to blend in all coastal-like
Despite our pasty skin and sensible practicalities
We were as out of place
As butchers at a PETA rally
We walked the great pier above the waves
While the locals fished in shorts and flip flops
On the beach we cast ourselves into the sea
I am nearly certain I was the only
Fifty-five year-old body surfer
In the entire Pacific that day
All the while not realizing that perhaps
I was teaching my eighteen-year-old
That a love for life has no age limit

BadAss Daddy

Despite his age
he was still a badass
in his old mind.
The beard he thought
made him look tough
was grey with distinction.
He rocked and rolled
to his 80s bands
at moderate volume,
was sure to hydrate
after binge drinking,
and stayed up late
sometimes until 11:00 PM.
His eight-year-old minivan
lacked boss headers
had uncool factory rims
and a laughable stereo
—also at moderate volume—
Yes, he was badass alright
listening to the Sex Pistols
while walking his terrier
in relaxed fit jeans
and comfortable shoes.

It Matters

Normally, it wouldn't be
a second thought;
a worm writhing
in the middle of
a hot sidewalk
desperate to reach
its grassy oasis.
I walked by it
continued on my way
but then stopped,
walked back
to the worm
and its writhingness,
picked it up
and tossed it
to the heavenly green
saving a worm life
or maybe not.

I'm not sure why
I stopped.

After all,
it was only a worm.
But I am at a point
in my life
where small things
seem like big things
like we're all part
of an aspirating life cycle
on a spinning piece of dirt
so I do what I can.

Bill of Health

I no longer go to the doctor
for a physical exam
expecting brevity
a handshake
and well wishes.
No.
Now I go with list in hand
to remind me
what hurts, bulges
sags, clicks, pops
oozes, throbs
gurgles, flakes,
starts when it shouldn't
or doesn't stop when it should.
This compilation of woes
gets heaped upon
the previously existing
ailment roster that
my doctor keeps around for
laughs with his colleagues
at happy hour.
I no longer come away
with advice to
keep doing what I've been doing
but rather
orders to *stop* doing
what I've been doing
along with
a prescription for pills
or an ointment,
a pamphlet about
fill-in-the-blank-itis

and warnings about
high blood pressure
alcoholic drinks
red meat, white meat,
meat in general
sugar
carbohydrates,
high fructose corn syrup
and too much white flour.
Yes, trips to the doctor
are not what they used to be.

Gunless Wonder

In gun-crazed America
I have not a gun
which probably makes me
a minority
a gunless freak
an unarmed anomaly
a victim in waiting.
None of this is to say
I never owned a gun
because I have,
a couple in fact.

Both were hunting shotguns
the first a double-barreled
nightmare prone to
synchronous firing
despite my pulling
only one trigger.
It was a disobedient beast
that left a dent in my shoulder
and led to my distrust
of flint, powder, fire and shot.

The second was a used
Remington pump model
that didn't seem to fire straight
couldn't hit the broad side
of a semi truck
from ten yards.

I eventually sold both
and used the money to buy
golf clubs when I turned 40.
Now my golf game looks
like I am driving the ball
using a shotgun.

Purgatorial Prose

I sit
mulling my next
poem
what should it be?
Starting with a blank page
its outcome lies somewhere
between Publication Limbo
Literary Purgatory
and Grammatical Gehenna
maybe I can pray it
into Poetic Paradise
I stare and stare
waiting for my tinnitus
to ring out inspiration
and bring salvation
nuanced nirvana
so I can move on
to my next
poem

Sixteen Times Four

The floor shakes with the bass
of my sixteen-year-old's
subwoofer.
Four boys in his room.
His buddies.
His *loud* buddies.
They're sixteen also.
And loud also.
I sit quietly enduring.

The big music
is spliced with
momentary electric guitar outbursts
by a friend who doesn't play
or maybe does
but not well.
This adds a layer
a level of chaos
to the already loud loudness,
making it louder.

He's come down twice.
Once for food,
once for water.
When the door opens
the loud escapes
and hits me
in my fifty-three-year-old face.
And it's become clear…

I've become the old man.

Terrestrially Adjusted

Tilted Thomas walks with a lean
of precisely
twenty-three point five degrees
which
it turns out
is exactly the tilt of
earth's axis.
He's terrestrially adjusted
rides a slanted bike
sits at a tilted desk in school
and is an excellent dancer
especially the limbo.
His fork is bent
to twenty-three point five
and he spills a fair amount of milk.
To us, he's leaning
but to him
we're leaning.
Please don't stare.
He's perfectly normal.

The Other Dean's List

My early college years
at the University of Minnesota
were spent shuffling majors
like a canasta deck.
Young and unfocused
freshman year
I floundered
flopping like a carp
on the banks
of the Mississippi.
My grades fluctuated
and flatulated
then haunted me like
an unpaid traffic ticket.
I was proficient
in poor study habits
reckless time management
and the social life
of a rock star.
My GPA recovery
was like extinguishing
the Hindenberg
with a squirt gun.
Fire is out.
One survivor.

Wading In

Our first child
found us
knee deep in
bottles and formula
nuks and binkies
sleepless nights
nap-filled days
soiled diapers
projectile yaks
onsies
toesies
ear infections
spit ups
and sippy cups.

When they grow
we get waist deep
in emotional outbursts
slammed doors
lost loves
oily skin
deep voices
armpit hair
too much cologne
broken curfews
privacy issues
high school dances
empty gas tanks
and turn that thing down!

ReCreation

On the eighth day, God took man and woman aside and asked what exactly they thought they were doing?
On the ninth day, God took all the non-extinct animals and gave them refuge.
On the tenth day, God dialed down the Sun's rays to offset man's global warming.
On the eleventh day, God ripped out the GMO Monsanto corn and filled in the open-pit mines.
On the twelfth day, God swept the sky clear of pollutants and sealed the hole in the ozone layer.
On the thirteenth day, God remade it ALL.
On the fourteenth day, He went to Disneyland.

Unqualified

The car needed more
than a poet could give.
Things like
metarotors and liquid love
a good dose of
traction diction
and heavy metal.
The poet channeled
his words and imagery
and slathered them
in an oily rhyme
and installed them
in the dyspeptic vehicle
but they just sat there
inertly with great defiance
and no visible
effect, except to make
the author feel better
about himself.
The car felt the same, though.
The poet sequestered
the assistance of his friends
who mopped up verses
from puddles of their
rejection and leftover
rusting stanzas
and sprayed them at
car of incorrigibility
to fruitless avail
so the poet divorced
himself from the
unfaithful machine,

annuled their vows
and started dating
a cheap port wine.

Unwelcome

Middle age came dressed in fat pants, slippers
and cheaters perched on its forehead.
When it showed up at my place
one day in December on my fiftieth birthday
it was wearing tendinitis like a bad necktie
had a small fortune in dental crowns
and constantly forgot what it left the room for.
Yes middle age was a rude fellow
he was not fond of change,
technology gave him fits
and he was prone to speaking his mind
even when not asked.
His hearing was failing and
he was addicted to vitamin supplements
to keep his joints loose, his veins supple
and his immunity on high alert.
I keep hoping middle age will leave
and let me get back to
living the life I used to live.
But he seems to have taken residence
with intentions of a long-term commitment.

Coffee and Crazy

A crazy guy came into
the coffee shop today.
He tried to hide it
but it stuck out
like a rodeo clown
in a monestary in Budapest
on Good Friday.
From his first sentence
to the barista
about the flat tire
that started his day
crazy spilled forth
and began consuming
all rational thought in the room.
It was a parasitical form
of crazy—feeding on sanity
like a tick bloated with crazy.
I recognized it immediately
as did others enjoying
their lucid, coherent coffee
with a dash of cream.
I managed to deflect
his interruptions
of craziness
by not establishing
eye contact, coupled with
a pair of ear buds
and a laptop
as my forcefield.
I was sporting a look
that said,

Move
your
crazy
along.
A sane couple
sitting nearby mistook
his introduction for simple
friendliness and spent
the next ten minutes
on the far side of crazy.

Created

God made us beautiful
the curious
the tempestuous
flirtatious
he made us
broken sometimes
bleeding
hurting ourselves
or others
made us
to love Him
each other
our neighbors
unequivocally
completely
freely
perfectly
leaving out
judgements
correction
made us
…

Continental Fake

The American tried to blend in
with the British locals
during his visit to London
hoping no one would notice him
or, even worse,
make the connection to his president
a man no longer welcome there.
But his gangly six-foot-four
Wisconsin frame
towered over the Londoners
in the subway car.
He stuck out like a sunflower
among dandelions
a California redwood among
the European ferns
so blending in was like
trying to hide a rhinoceros
in a Kmart shoebox.
Then there was his dialect
which sounded like a
a cross between Canadian
throat singing and
Gregorian plain chant.
It wasn't all chip-chip
and cheerio
which tipped his hand
every time he opened his mouth.
His Yankee-ness
clung to him like a
lycra tuxedo on a drag queen.
Yes, there was no denying
his McDonald heritage

he was a Milli Vanilli European
faking it
hoping no one would
stop the music.

Character and Charm

The bathroom sink drains slowly
the water dragging its feet
and griping about too much hair
while in the kitchen
the dishwasher chokes
on its own vomit like a
dying rockstar.

Up on the roof
the incontinent chimney
wets itself again
causing embarrassing stains
on the ceiling of its pants.
In the cellar the furnace
belches its displeasure
and regurgitates
last year's air upon us.

Nothing is plumb
or square,
or flush,
or sealed,
efficient, new,
or up to code.
Most of it needs attention.
This geriatric home
could use some living assistance.

Asocial Media

The Twitter Troll
didn't know me
but trolled me
like he did.

The Facebook Fiend
lashed out loud
drubbed with words
forced an unfollowing.

The Linked-In Loser
connected for reasons
that seemed noble
but got him nowhere.

The Instagram Ignoramus
pictured his life
only to show
it was unfocused.

A Triage of Words

The heart of our
Monday writers' group
is the improper
alignment of words,
herniated pronouns,
sentence fragments,
and their long-winded cousins
the run ons.
Sometimes we tell and don't show
while the "word of the week"
spurts like an artery
and cancerous semicolons
beg for removal.
With the care of
a surgical team,
we slice, remove,
stitch and elevate
the wounded words until
the page stops bleeding
the color returns
and the patient shows the
illusory promise of
life on its own.

Sign Here, Here and Here

The Office of Unintended Government Bureaucracy
specializes in not-quite-forward thinking.
It is certainly not leading-edge
more like flailing edge.
It requires forms, signatures and authorizations,
user fees, legal counsel, and clearances,
carbon copies, statements of intent, and affadavits,
proof of identification, ten day waiting periods, written permission,
birth certificates, proofs of residency, death certificates,
appeals, certifications, notary public witness,
and even letters from other government bureaucrats.
Telling folks what they can do
often means telling them more things they cannot do.
The most curious thing is how anything gets done at all.

A Drop in the Bucket

The drop was part of a Great Flood
that lasted forty days
then percolated to an aquifer,
was drawn from a well,
stored in a jar and turned to wine.
It reappeared as an ice crystal
on the beard of
a Federal soldier
during the bitter winter
in Valley Forge.
Years later it showed up as a tear
on the cheek of Jaqueline Kennedy
in a church in 1963.
It evaporated and became part of a storm cloud
that rained into the Cuyahoga river
where it caught fire in Cleveland
and was extinguished
by fellow drops
then rolled over Niagara Falls
without a barrel.
After a trip to Europe
and a pint of Guiness
it snowed down
on top of Mount Everest.
Later the drop crossed the Pacific
and ended up in Dean Martin's pool.
After a dip, it rode the Jet Stream as a cloud
West to Lake Superior
where it helped sink the Edmund Fitzgerald.

Disorderly Lives

We race and chase and push
and shove and text and dial and shout
and schmooze and spend and splurge
to get things that make us more in our own eyes.

Then we cook and shop and boil and bake
and gulp and chomp and burp and slurp
and sip and guzzle and grind and swallow
to taste the goodness of life before us.

Then we play and work and wander
and drive and bike and walk
and run and rush and ride
to get us out of here and now.

Then we retire and relax and regurgitate
and reminisce and rejoice and remember,
and reflect and repeat and recall
all of the things we might have done.

Then we get old and slow and feeble
and deaf and opinionated and cranky
and stubborn and sick and tired
and die knowing life was complete.

Count to Five

The germs from the floor
upon which I dropped my toast
are surely benign, I think,
as I pick up the jellied piece
which gratefully
and gracefully,
landed
face
up.

Five second rule.

Filling Space

The metal in my mouth
picks up space signals
which come in an alien language
a mixture of Brazilian Portuguese
and Latin
sprinkled with political lies
in plain English.

I talked to my dentist about this
he said that I had two options:
I could move to Brazil
assimilate and learn a dead language
to decipher the messages.

Or, I could get crowns
in place of all my metal fillings
so the messages would stop.

Foi uma escolha fácil   (*It was an easy choice*
quia non sum sicut dentists b*ecause I do not like dentist*s)
Read my lips,
I did not have sexual relations
with that woman.

Downriver

I stared death in
its rotting fish eyes
during a swim on a river
whose current
stared me down
then pulled me down
tried to hold me down
little by little
I was
going
down.

The water was cooler
than July's baking sun
making it
a better place to die
but at seventeen
I wasn't quite ready
had a few things
I still wanted to do
I wasn't
quite
ready.

I fought the current
like a drunken bitch
in a cat fight
flailing and thrashing
but that old river
just rolled and laughed
sapping my strength
bit by bit

It was
taking
me.

A friend who didn't
want me to die
pulled me from the river's
watery death clutches
kicked that thing
right in the head
said, "This is my friend!"
and dragged me in
He was
saving
me.

My sister has dreamed
a half dozen times
that I've died
in drowning accidents
horrifying nightmares
and while it hasn't
happened yet
I have a feeling
I am
destined
to.

Incarnaturalization

The white guy lived in Michigan
working a blue collar job
and living squarely in the middle class
his whole life, until his death at 54
when his spirit returned as an Indian Sikh
with an arm gnarled by a textile machine.
He was a third world rendition of himself
until he had an aneurysm while sleeping
and his karma reappeared as a Spanish woman
a widow with six children in a small house
holding two jobs as waitress and maid
surrounded by strife, toil and the love of family
before she fell broke her hip
and died of an infection at sixty-four.

There are six billion souls on earth
but one spirit redesigning itself
over and over and over
resulting in a
completely
unique
you.

Don't waste it.

Talking Around the Problem

When geometry takes a backseat
to active shooting drills
and lockdown exercises.
We could have us a gun problem.

Or, when the student body
means one lying in the classroom
instead of the corporate whole.
We may have a gun problem.

Maybe when the suggested solution
to stopping the next school assassin
is to arm the English teacher.
We might just have us a gun problem.

If people speak about knives and bricks
as potential weapons of mass murder
"So are we going to ban those too?"
We certainly appear to have a gun problem.

When students become survivors
and stand up to NRA politicians
but still laws don't change.
It's safe to say we have a gun problem.

Heaven

I wonder what heaven will be like.
Will it be all strawberry fields forever
or hello yellow brick road?
Will it feel like a roller coaster at the fair
or a canoe ride down a lazy creek?
I'm sure people expect different things.
Some will want it to smell like chocolate chip cookies
others will prefer the scent of a distant campfire.
My choice is cookies.
I wonder if time will feel the same?
Will a two hour movie last fourteen years
or a three minute egg take ten seconds?
Is the temperature going to be just right
or too hot, too cold, too drafty, too stifling?
Might a person be able to get a stiff drink
or a good strong cup of coffee
with endless refills and no caffeine shakes?
Is heaven going to be like the library
or more like Grand Central Station?
Will there be a dress code
or come as you are?
I wonder.

Grand

On the avenue of our youth
where retail danced with residential
neither the apparent lead
but rather a tolerant equality,
cars boxed out the bikes
and buses returned the favor to cars.
I was sent to this street with a note
from my big sister posing as mother
for a minor cigarette purchase
from a skeptical drug store clerk.
I squandered my quarter payment
on hits of sugar coated glee
or paperboard sports heroes
with rectangles of stale gum.
It was the road to our coming of age
the pathway of our first jobs
routing us through life.
But forty years later
our street wears thick glasses
skinny jeans and a lumberjack beard
drinks expensive coffee
named with long pretentious words
and stares into its phone
grinning at cat videos.

Son

I want him
to ride his bike off of jumps he made himself,
climb perilous escarpments for no good reason,
and sneak into an event without paying.

I hope he
plays with fireworks without getting hurt,
tries smoking, but decides it's not his thing,
and drives 100 MPH just to say he did.

I wish he
would clean his room unprovoked,
stop jumping out and scaring me
and turn that damn thing down.

I expect he
will open doors for dates,
stick up for a friend,
and move back home for a time after college.

I think he
has the carefree spirit of his father,
the conscience of his mother,
and is uniquely and unequivocally, himself.

Family Medicine

One would think that a straight, white, college-educated, Christian male with a wife of twenty-seven years, two honor student children, a government job, a house in the suburbs, a dog, two cats, two cars, a kayak, three laptops, a pension *and* 457b and a pretty decent health care plan would have it made.

But with all of those things come white privilege guilt, crushing compassion for the marginalized, a questioning of his faith, gender shame, parental second-guessing, fears of job loss, self- esteem issues, dark days, regrets, environmental empathy, self-loathing, a mountain of debt and all the dread and insecurities that comes with it.

We are all waging personal wars within ourselves. Even the world's most confident, upbeat, optimistic, gifted person ducks from occasional rounds fired from their own mind. So before I judge or envy this man or that woman, I revisit the battleground upon which I lay bleeding from my latest self-inflicted wounds and find family applying healing pressure like a tourniquet.

Fighting Words

The words take many forms
the brevity of a poem
the punchline of a knock knock joke
the long-winded political bill
and the Sincerely Yours of a letter.

And nothing mean they taken
when context out of or
jumbledtogetherlikewordsalad.

If u luk @ words on a phone
they might hive been changed
by autocoercion to mane
sometime unattended.

And sometimes your friends
will get there possessives wrong
and loose there English credibility
while you're sure their there
was meant to be they're.

While some might hate English
with it's dizzying grammatical rules
and all of its regional colloquialisms
I have grown to love it
like an old, somewhat annoying friend.

The Face of Rain

The rainstorm ruins a picnic in Wisconsin
Acts like a monsoon in Pakistan
Poses as a hurricane in New Orleans
Turns to snow in Minnesota
And ices into sleet in Kentucky
It's part of the routine in Seattle
And beats the odds in Vegas
Is a no-show in Death Valley
And is captured and held hostage in Los Angeles

Giants

They spoke in
muffled bass tones
but they spoke,
the sequoias did.
They talked about
the good old days
four hundred years ago
when Native Americans
admired them for beauty
and their ancient spirit.
I felt privileged
to be among them
they welcomed me
whispering softly
among the low ferns
where I swear
a few even laughed
raspy old tree laughs
happy ancient giants
watching yet another
generation pass below.

A Look Around

I watch my young son
careen through the living room
like a baby dragon
on a five hour energy drink
sneezing fire like
napalm snot rockets
that singe the cat
with kerosene authority
and a level of preschool
righteousness, he is
a prehistoric demolitionist
in potty training pants.

I listen to my daughter
whose thoughts
race in the demolition
derby pit of her mind
ten years ahead
of her ability to
articulate them.
Her thoughts
are smoking hulks
dead in the corner
while drivers curse
spin their tires
and slam steering wheels
in frustration.

Meanwhile my brain
sputters and sparks
like a microwave fire
just out of reach
of the baking soda.

Thoughts come and go
passing each other
unseatbelted
without signaling
flipping one another off
and driving under the
influence of last month's
bad decisions.

Dreamscape

I have a dream
it comes wrapped in small satchel
tied with barbed wire.
I have a satchel
and in it is
the answer to my question.
I have a question
that can only be answered
by admitting my vices.
I have vices
that would make
a convict look innocent.
I have an innocence
that betrays the trust
I laid before you.
I have you
and you have me
and we have each other.
I have an other
that is different from
that which I left.
I have differences
between what I feel
and what I see.
I have seen
the unspeakable actions
of angry people.
I have anger
that I repress
into my dreams.
I have dreams.

Flattened

He looked at the flattened
toothpaste tube rolled as a
desperate attempt at getting
something for nothing but
you can't get blood from a stone
nor paste from last week's life
that was lived like there was
no tomorrow; well today is
that reality just like the
half empty tissue box plays
a minor part in the bathroom
theater of his mometary cameo
on a gigantic fragile peanut M&M
with a thin, but melting layer
of ozone and a molten center.
So he pours himself a cup of
afternoon clarity born on
a Nicaraguan mountainside
shape shifting from solid to
liquid during its journey from
south to north, then down
the hatch, rented then
expelled like a cheap date
giving bad directions home
and hoping for a kiss
but getting only a firm
handshake and a coupon
for tomorrow's day old bread.

Quiet One

He was a man of few words
where most people just blurted forth
his words tossed around in his head
like a brain salad of consonants and vowels
waiting for a chance to form themselves
into bold, assertive sentences of wisdom
but never quite finding the right
time, opportunity or audience.

To him the unspoken thought
was as natural as
putting on pants or making coffee
only with considerably less effort.
Plus, he thought there were enough words
being spoken in the world
without adding his to the glut
bringing the value of all of them down
and there's some truth to that.

Because of this affliction
or character defect, or gift
depending on how you look at it
people assumed that when he spoke
his words were filled with wisdom.
They weren't.
He was just releasing word pressure
from his salad spinner because it hurt
and even a man of few words
has opinions now and then.

House Arrest

Its given name is Polar Vortex
apparently some sort of practical joke
hold-my-beer-moment by Old Man Winter
intended to rid the Midwest of
the weak, infirm and underdressed.
It rolls into the northern states
throwing its frosty weight around
like it owns the place
which it pretty much does
like a slumlord with a drinking problem.
Vortex will freeze you out with no mercy
bringing his uninvited windbag cousin
blowing saxophones of feels-like
at varying degrees of negativity.

The Fourth of July before the End of the World

The fourth of July fell on the third this year
in part because of the whole leap year on
a Wednesday thing. It was a product
of the new world paradigm brought
forward by American leadership ill-equipped
to anticipate disasters
such
as
this.

Every Tuesday afternoon came after sunset
as well, the darkness setting in around
two o'clock and staying until after
dark, sometimes it stayed until
Wednesday evening when it
got
light
again.

Easter fell on St. Patrick's day which
this year was a Saturday during advent
or maybe during Chanukah, in any case
it was some form of religious holiday
but certainly not the one Patrick
nor his snakes intended
it
to
be.

The end of the world came unannounced
on a Monday of a three day weekend
when most of the world's men and a few women
were sleeping or making morning coffee
it was horribly inconvenient timing for the end
of
the
world.

Shelf Life

The shelf of unwritten books awaits you
it sits there, empty, bleary eyed
unable to blink
thinking about the possible endings
to the story you meant to write
but can't seem to get around to.
The shelf mourns and weeps
for the authors who never wrote
those stories of love, addiction
courage and broken characters
it weeps pages and pages of tears
shaped like apostrophes of sadness.
One day the shelf dreamed of your book
as you talked excitedly about
your new work in progress
like it was the latest girlfriend
with hair braided of words.
So far you'd numbered all the pages
picked a title and even sketched her a cover.
But the shelf of unwritten books
still lays there flat, alone and celibate
a spinster shelf
waiting for that hopeful someday
that may yet never come
because the idea of a book
is much easier than birthing one.

Lion

The lion that roared in my youth
has become a circus clown wearing
humility and dark shades of self-doubt.
It has forsaken recklessness and kisses
in the name of frugality, passenger side air bags
and a healthy sense of mortality.
Instead of risk and deliverance
it compresses my spine and
sings using the wrong lyrics.
We talked over expensive, six-word coffee
about Jesus, John Lennon, Mahara-ji
and that time we drank too much.
Now, when dusk sets in and the moon
takes its place in the astral coatroom
I see a Cheshire cat grin in the mirror.

This Is a Test

As I sit in the soundproof booth
I wonder why I am here
staring at the oddly situated
statue of Minnie Mouse
on the ledge in the corner
which sparks the question,
was Minnie deaf?

You'll hear ascending tones
the audiologist said
handing me the clicker
Click when the sound starts
I wait a long time for the first
or maybe it had already begun?
I clicked anyway – just in case.

Next you'll hear sentences – repeat them
This will be easier for me, I'm certain.
The man walks down the lit garden path.
The ocean waves crash on the shore.
A party on the iceberg was full of cat chow.
The hot log spender pouted proudly.
…something about a horse.

Next will be sentences with increasing background noise
Uh oh, this could get ugly.
Repeat all or as much of the sentence as you can
She has a shiny red convertible car
They drank the occupied territory incompletely
The mouse had colon pewter pancakes
…something about frozen somethings

When the test was complete
the doctor looked at me gravely
like she had just heard an alien language
which indeed she had
she looked at me like I was old
which indeed I was
and I began to understand why I was there.

About the Author

Jim has three books of poetry, *Written Life, Reciting from Memory* and *On a Road*. He also has two memoirs, *Dirty Shirt: A Boundary Waters Memoir* and *The Portland House: A '70s Memoir*. His nonfiction stories have been published in *Main Street Rag, Prairie Rose Publications, Steam Ticket, Story News,* and others. He lives in Waukesha, Wisconsin with his wife, Donna. He enjoys fishing, kayaking, biking, and camping. Jim is poet laureate for the Village of Wales, Wisconsin. For more on his writing, visit: http://jimlandwehr.com